MW01063056

BOARD MEMBER ORIENTATION

The Concise and Complete Guide to
NONPROFIT BOARD SERVICE

MICHAEL E. BATTS

Accountability
Press

www.accountabilitypress.com

in cooperation with

www.nonprofitcpa.com

Copyright © 2011 Michael E. Batts
All rights reserved.

ISBN: 1-4563-0491-7
ISBN-13: 978-1-4563-0491-1

This book is dedicated to my wonderful and beautiful wife, Karen, who has been my number one supporter, helper, best friend, and the sunshine in my life for more than 28 years. What accomplishments I have been blessed to have achieved would not have been possible without God's providence and the incredible support of my wife. I am also incredibly grateful for the support, interest, encouragement, entertainment, and humor that our four awesome children, Monica, Michael, Christopher, and Clayton, have supplied during the writing of this book. Without them, some of the long days would have been much longer and much less enjoyable.

Acknowledgments

I would like to express my sincere gratitude to the people who provided editorial assistance and wise advice to me in the writing of this book.

First, I would like to thank Dan Busby, President of ECFA, and a true mentor, for his wise insights on topics related to board governance and the format of the book.

Todd Chasteen, a good friend and General Counsel for Samaritan's Purse, provided extensive and thoughtful input related to legal matters addressed in the book, for which I am deeply grateful.

I am truly grateful to Doug Starcher, a good friend and a partner with the law firm of Broad and Cassel, for his invaluable assistance with intellectual property matters and with certain legal topics addressed in the book.

My friend, Dr. Frank Wright, President of National Religious Broadcasters, also provided excellent insights, especially in areas related to board member communications, for which I am most grateful.

I would like to thank Chuck Hartman, Associate Professor of Business Law and Accounting at Cedarville University, for his excellent commentary on elements of the book to facilitate learning and retention of the topics presented.

My fellow shareholders, Kim Morrison, Michele Wales, and Mike Lee, provided extraordinary editorial assistance and excellent suggestions for improving the book's clarity in a number of areas. Jennifer Marshall and Andrea Martinez, my executive assistants, also provided excellent help with editing and a variety of logistics. Thank you all, team. You are awesome.

I would also like to express profound gratitude to all of the clients of our firm, who are also our friends, and who provide the inspiration for this work.

Table of Contents

Introduction
i

Using This Book for Board Member Orientation
iii

1. The Legal Authority and Responsibility of Board Members
Page 1

2. The Proper Role of the Board
Page 7

3. Board Committees
Page 15

4. The Board's Role in Risk Management
Page 21

5. The Board's Role in Financial Matters
Page 27

6 . Governing and Policy Documents
Page 35

7. The Liability of Board Members
Page 47

8. Understanding, Evaluating, and Protecting Mission
Page 53

9. Board Meeting Dynamics
Page 59

*10. Completing the Orientation Process by Providing
Organization-Specific Information to Board Members*
Page 69

Introduction

Serving on a nonprofit board can be an incredibly rewarding experience. And, unless there is something highly unusual about the organization, serving on the board does not have to be complicated. This book is for the generous and busy people who agree to give of their time and talents by serving on nonprofit boards. Nonprofit boards often fail to do a good job of board member orientation for a variety of reasons. It takes a significant amount of time and effort to plan and conduct quality board member orientation programs, and every time a new board member arrives, it is time to do it again. What's more, unless a nonprofit board has in-house experts in the field of nonprofit board governance, the information provided in such orientation sessions may be lacking in quality, accuracy, or completeness. Because of the challenges associated with providing quality board member orientation, many nonprofit organizations don't do it at all, leaving their board members to "wing it." Responsible nonprofit board members generally prefer not to wing it when it comes to the serious matter of board service.

Hooey Alerts!

When nonprofit board members and leaders do seek information about the world of nonprofit board governance, one unfortunate result is that the information they receive is often wrong. There are many purveyors of false or misleading information about the nonprofit board service environment. A perfect example is the often vaguely worded and intimidating assertion or implication that the *Sarbanes-Oxley Act* passed by Congress in 2002 applies to nonprofit organizations in a manner similar to how it applies to publicly-traded companies. (It doesn't. That is an example of **hooey** – *false or misleading information, malarkey, or bunk*.) Occasionally in this book, I have inserted **Hooey Alerts!** to warn the reader of misinformation that is common related to the topic at hand.

After chairing, serving on, and consulting with nonprofit boards for more than 25 years, I have concluded that nonprofit boards and their members could benefit from a concise, accurate, and appropriately comprehensive book about nonprofit board service. In order to be truly helpful, such a book must be sufficiently brief to allow a busy executive to read it in short order – maybe on an airplane flight. (A number of excellent books have been written about nonprofit board governance, covering most relevant topics in significant detail. Many of them are hundreds of pages long. Very few nonprofit board members have the time to read such lengthy works.) The book must also address with accuracy the most significant elements of board service, such as mission, responsibility, duty, risk, liability, and board meeting dynamics.

It is my sincere hope that this book will provide help and support to some of the truly great men and women serving on nonprofit boards because their service makes a positive difference in the lives of countless people every day.

Mike Batts

Using This Book for Board Member Orientation

The primary objective of this book is to facilitate nonprofit board member orientation. An orientation process must address two essential components:

- General information about the world of nonprofit board service, and

- Specific information about the unique attributes of the organization being served.

General information about board service

Chapters 1-9 of this book are designed to provide board members with an overview of the general aspects of nonprofit board service.

Information specific to your organization

Chapter 10 is designed to help you complete the orientation process by facilitating communication with board members about information that is specific to your organization.

A complete curriculum!

When following the steps suggested in Chapter 10, this book can serve as a complete board member orientation curriculum for your organization.

1
The Legal Authority and Responsibility of Board Members

This book is written with the assumption that your nonprofit organization is a corporation, which is the case for the vast majority of nonprofit organizations in the United States. The main principles would apply, however, to nonprofits organized as trusts or other less common types of legal entities.

U.S. nonprofit corporations are legal entities formed pursuant to the laws of one of the states in the United States. Each state's laws contain specific statutes governing the activities of nonprofit (or "not-for-profit") corporations. The nonprofit corporation statutes of all states contain a roughly equivalent version of the following:

> All corporate powers must be exercised by or under the authority of, and the affairs of the corporation managed under the direction of, its board of directors, subject to any limitation set forth in the articles of incorporation. *(Section 617.0801, Florida Statutes)*

In other words, **the board of directors of a nonprofit corporation has full and final authority over the affairs of the organization,** unless the organization's articles of incorporation limit the board's authority in some way. (Such a limitation might exist, for example, when an organization has voting members and the articles of incorporation reserve for the membership the right to amend the articles of incorporation.)

Given this full and final authority over the affairs of an organization, the board is, then, ultimately responsible for overseeing and directing the activities of the organization. The board's authority and responsibility apply to every aspect of an organization's operations and activities.

Some nonprofit boards act as if they do not realize or accept the fact that they possess this full and final authority over and responsibility for all of their organization's activities. Instead, they act as if they are merely advisors to the president or CEO of the organization. The board has authority over all staff and all activities of the organization and as a matter of law must recognize that fact and act accordingly. The board must be fully engaged in its role as such.

In the wake of some of the recent financial scandals involving U.S. nonprofit organizations, Senator Charles Grassley – former Chairman of the U.S. Senate Finance Committee – expressed great frustration over the fact that the boards of the organizations in question seemed not to realize or act upon their authority and responsibility as the "gatekeepers" of the organizations, especially with respect to the activities of the CEOs.

In a particularly noteworthy and scathing floor speech on March 19, 2007, Senator Grassley excoriated the Smithsonian

Institution's Secretary (CEO) and board for making lavish expenditures including:

- Hundreds of thousands of dollars on renovations and decorating of the Secretary's home,

- $13,000 for a conference table,

- Thousands of dollars for a trip to Las Vegas for the Secretary and his wife, and

- Chauffeured limousine services.

Near the end of his speech, Grassley made the following statement addressing the manner in which the Smithsonian's board had handled the matter when such expenditures were first brought to light:

> *"...it raises very real concerns in my mind of whether the Board is running the Smithsonian and its Secretary or whether the Secretary is running the Board."*

No individual authority

It is also very important to note that the authority and responsibility of the board of directors exists only as a body, and not for individual board members. Individual board members do not have authority to direct the affairs or actions of the organization unless specific authority to represent the board with respect to specific matters has been vested in them by the board itself or by the organization's governing documents.

The fiduciary duty of individual board members

Board members each have a "fiduciary duty" with respect to overseeing the organization's activities. The fiduciary duty of a board member encompasses the duty of care, the duty of loyalty, and the duty of obedience.

The duty of care

The duty of care requires a board member to act in good faith, in a manner he or she reasonably believes to be in the best interests of the organization, and with the care an ordinarily prudent person would exercise in a like position under similar circumstances.

The duty of loyalty

The duty of loyalty requires a board member to act in the best interests of the organization rather than in his own interests or in the interests of his associates. For example, a board member who learns of a real estate investment opportunity during one of the nonprofit's board meetings may not seize the opportunity personally to the disadvantage of the organization. The duty of loyalty also requires the board member to avoid or fully disclose potential conflicts of interest by complying with the organization's conflicts-of-interest policy as described below. It also encompasses maintaining appropriate confidentiality.

The duty of obedience

The duty of obedience requires a board member to comply with applicable laws and to act in conformity with the organization's governing and policy documents.

Conflicts of interest

Board members that have conflicts of interest with the organization in connection with business transactions must be careful to follow appropriate procedures in addressing such transactions. For example, if a board member owns a construction company that the organization is considering hiring to perform a construction project, the board member has a conflict of interest with respect to the proposed transaction. Nonprofit organizations should have a good conflicts-of-interest policy that addresses such situations by requiring procedures similar to the following:

- The conflicted board member is excused from discussion (other than preliminary discussions to help other board members understand the facts) and voting on the matter;

- The board members without a conflict (or a committee thereof) evaluate comparability data (such as competing bids, appraisals, etc.) to determine that the terms of the transaction would be fair market value or better to the organization;

- The board or committee determines whether it believes the transaction would be in the best interests of the organization (assuming the terms are determined to be fair value or better); and

- The board or committee members vote on the transaction and record their decision (and the basis for it) contemporaneously in the minutes of the board or committee.

The Internal Revenue Service has published on its website (www.irs.gov) a model conflicts-of-interest policy that serves as a useful guide for nonprofit organizations in developing their own policies.

Executive Recap

- The board has full and final authority over the affairs of the organization.

- Some boards do not realize or accept that fact.

- Board members have authority only as a body and not individually.

- Board members have a fiduciary duty to the organization that encompasses the duty of care, the duty of loyalty, and the duty of obedience.

- The board must have and follow a good conflicts-of-interest policy.

2
The Proper Role of the Board

While the board has full authority over and responsibility for overseeing the affairs of the nonprofit organization, that does not mean, of course, that the board must carry out all the work of the organization. In fact, the board should not be involved at all in the operational activities of the organization unless it is a very small organization with little or no staff.

Thou shalt not

Various authors, consultants, and groups in the United States espouse a variety of governance styles and practices. There are plenty of excellent resources available on the finer points of governance styles and "best practices" as determined by the respective authors. However, proponents of virtually all styles of board governance generally agree on one fundamental principle: **boards and board members should not micromanage the affairs of the organization**. To do so is to leave the board table and take on the role of management. The reason this proscription is so important has nothing to do with the board's <u>actual</u> authority. As we have already clearly established, the board has complete authority over the affairs of the organization, so it may take on whatever role it chooses. Rather, a board must refrain from engaging in operating activities in order to ensure that the organization is functional – as opposed to being *dys*functional. Engagement by board members in the operating affairs of an organization undermines the authority of the president or CEO of the organization. When a board hires a CEO to lead an organization, of necessity, it must give the CEO the authority to actually run the organization, free from interference. When the board entangles itself in the daily decision-making process, a CEO never knows where the lines of authority start and stop. A good CEO will not tolerate such an environment and will seek escape from it as soon as possible. Of course, when board members choose to entangle themselves in management, they also lose sight of the lines of authority. Clearly, such an arrangement is dysfunctional.

Thou shalt

You are probably familiar with the acronym "SOP" for "standard operating procedure." That acronym is useful as a reminder of the key areas of proper board action in a well-governed organization – strategy, oversight, and policy.

Strategy

The board is responsible for establishing the general strategy of the organization – what it seeks to accomplish, its mission, purpose, and objectives. The board should articulate such items in clear language, starting with a mission statement that effectively communicates what the organization considers to be its calling. The mission statement can be enhanced and supplemented with more specific statements and/or strategic plans developed by the board together with the organization's top management.

Strategy also includes mapping out the financial plan, or budget, for carrying out the organization's mission. Chapter 5 is dedicated to the board's role with respect to the financial affairs of an organization.

The strategy element of a board's role also includes ensuring that the organization is led by an effective CEO capable of carrying out the organization's mission and purposes. It is often said that the single most important role of the nonprofit board is the hiring and oversight of the CEO.

Oversight

Oversight by the board encompasses monitoring and evaluating all aspects of the organization's activities, including but not limited to:

- Ensuring adherence to the organization's mission and purposes (avoiding "mission drift");

- Evaluating the effectiveness with which the organization is carrying out its mission and purposes;

- Evaluating the performance of, establishing the compensation of, and encouraging the CEO;

- Evaluating compliance with the organization's governing documents and with applicable laws and regulations;

- Evaluating the funding and financial condition of the organization; and

- Ensuring that the organization maintains adequate risk management.

When the board identifies a deficiency in any of its areas of oversight, the properly governed board takes one of two courses of action or a combination of the two – holding the CEO accountable or modifying policy.

If the deficiency involves effectiveness or adherence to strategy, policy, or the law, the board has only one place to look – to the CEO. The board must hold the CEO accountable for the organization's overall effectiveness in carrying out its mission and in adhering to the law, as well as the organization's board-established strategies and policies. In a well-governed organization, the CEO and only the CEO, is held accountable directly by the board. A deficiency caused by the ineffectiveness of another member of the staff should be addressed by the CEO or his/her designee, but the board holds the CEO ultimately accountable, just as the law holds the board ultimately accountable. The board should also serve as a source of encouragement and support to the CEO who is performing well.

Policy

When a deficiency is identified that relates to the organization's policies themselves, the well-governed board will take prudent steps to evaluate and modify policy as necessary. Policy in this context refers to every element of board-approved guidance, including but not limited to the mission or purpose statement, articles of incorporation, bylaws, and board-approved policies. Chapter 6 is dedicated to the topic of board policy and the hierarchy of governing documents.

The sometimes fuzzy line between the proper role of the board and micromanagement

There are times, even with a well-governed organization, when the line between proper board oversight and dysfunctional micromanagement becomes a bit blurred.

For example, assume an organization's highly effective CEO decides to embark upon a new strategy to raise revenue by opening a thrift store. Nothing in the organization's policies prohibits the operation of a thrift store, and after performing some due diligence, the CEO opens a thrift store near the organization's headquarters. While generally very happy with the CEO's overall performance, several board members consider the thrift store to be an embarrassment to the organization and seek to have the thrift store closed as a board action item. As you can imagine from this example, a number of important dynamics come into play, not the least of which is the rapport and communication between the CEO and the board. A wise board facing such a dilemma will not reprimand an otherwise excellent CEO over a rather innocuous matter, but it may not be able to ignore the operating issue either. Such occasional circumstances must be handled with wisdom and care, and as long as they are, indeed, occasional, they are not a cause for great concern.

Another common scenario in which the line may become a bit blurred is in the strategic planning process. Strategic planning meetings involving the board and the CEO typically include brainstorming sessions in which various ideas are tossed around regarding the organization's strategies, goals, activities, and other similar topics. Invariably, board members participating in such discussions will offer the CEO ideas and suggestions regarding operational matters, often on the fly. Such exchanges are expected and can constitute a healthy discussion process if handled correctly. When sharing ideas about operational matters, both the board members and the CEO must remember that board members have no individual authority and the board as a whole will not take action on operating matters. So long as such discussions are handled accordingly, they can be immensely helpful to all involved and are not a cause for concern.

The role of the board in fundraising

Fundraising is a critically important activity for nonprofit organizations that depend on donations or grants as a significant source of funding. It is common practice among nonprofit charities to expect their boards to be very active in the fundraising process and to be significant donors themselves. Participation by board members in fundraising activities can be a very positive aspect of their volunteer service to the organization. In a high-profile charity, serving on the board is sometimes considered a position of status in the community that is awarded to the organization's major donors. Organizations following such a practice sometimes refer to their boards as "fundraising boards." For some organizations, the culture of maintaining a "fundraising board" causes the board not to realize or focus on their actual legal responsibilities as the governing body of the organization. In this type of environment, board meetings can become little more than pleasant social occasions peppered with "feel good" reports from management. Regardless of an organization's expectation of board members with respect to fundraising, nonprofit board members should remember that the board's primary legal responsibility is to govern the organization and oversee its activities. The board must be fully engaged in its role as such.

An organization may not simply decide to change the primary role of its board from one of oversight to one focused on fundraising. Failure to realize this important point creates an environment conducive to the board becoming passive with respect to its legal responsibilities or becoming effectively subordinate to management. Most of the financial scandals that occur in nonprofit organizations arise out of such an environment.

An organization that currently operates with a "fundraising board" approach and wishes to change to a true board governance model should consider forming an ad hoc committee (see the description of committees in Chapter 3) to recommend to the board the necessary changes to correct the situation. The material in this book may serve as a useful tool in the conversion process.

Executive Recap

- The board should not micromanage the affairs of the organization.

- The board's proper role is to focus on strategy, oversight, and policy matters.

- Arguably, the board's most important role is hiring and oversight of the CEO.

- Occasionally, the line between the board's proper role and improper micromanagement may become blurred, and such situations must be handled with care.

- Expectations of board members with respect to fundraising activities should be defined clearly.

- An organization's board cannot shirk its legal responsibility and become simply a "fundraising board" that does not have oversight responsibility for the organization.

3
Board Committees

Nonprofit boards often utilize committees to assist the board in carrying out specific elements of its work. It is very common, however, for boards to have committees or committee structures that are dysfunctional. The primary reason a nonprofit organization may have dysfunctional board committees is that the board itself has no clear conceptual framework for evaluating or determining the need for a specific committee or its objectives.

In speaking at various conferences and workshops nationally on nonprofit board governance topics, I often ask participants, "What is your organization's basis for determining whether you need a board committee to address a specific area such as finance, personnel, or any other area?" I have yet to receive a clear and cohesive answer to the question. Boards often tend to create standing committees such as finance committees, audit committees, and development (fundraising) committees because they think it is the thing to do...because they know of other organizations that have them. Some create an audit committee because they are victims of *hooey* and believe it is required by the IRS or the *Sarbanes-Oxley Act.* (It is not.)

Nonprofit boards should have a conceptual framework for determining if and when a board committee is needed. The framework must keep in mind the proper role of the board as we addressed in Chapter 2. A board committee is not an operations group. For example, a committee that engages in fundraising activities, public relations, or event planning is not (or should not be) a board committee. Such a group is an operating or activity committee that should operate under the authority of the CEO and management. Since boards should limit their activity to the areas of strategy, oversight, and policy, the same should be true of the board's committees; otherwise they will be dysfunctional.

Committee charters

No board should have any committee without a very clear charter setting forth the objectives and responsibilities of the committee. Without a clear charter, board committees will likely have a difficult time discerning whether an issue or a decision is within the scope of their responsibility or authority. Such confusion contributes greatly to dysfunctional board governance. A committee charter should be approved by the full board.

Committee authority

Board committees are rarely vested with authority to act on behalf of the full board. Much more commonly, board committees address specific board-level issues in more detail than the full board wishes to do itself and then makes recommendations to the full board.

The executive committee

A common exception to this general rule involves the use of an executive committee. Many organizations maintain a standing executive committee that is vested with authority to act on behalf of the full board in certain circumstances. Some organizations authorize the executive committee to act in the board's stead between full board meetings whenever the committee deems it appropriate or expedient. Others permit the executive committee to act on behalf of the full board in emergency situations, and still others vest the executive committee with board-level authority with respect to certain decisions (for example, setting executive compensation). The composition of the executive committee varies by organization, but many organizations with executive committees stipulate in their bylaws that the organization's officers comprise the executive committee.

The decision as to whether an executive committee is helpful or needed, and if so, what level of authority it should have, should not be made lightly. Advocates of utilizing an executive committee tout the expediency factor and the ability to act promptly when needed. There are, however, some distinct risks associated with utilizing an executive committee. One such risk is that the executive committee could become a miniature board within the board, which often creates a perception that the executive committee is the center of real board authority. Such a perception can alienate board members who are not on the executive committee, or make them feel like "second-class board members."

Another risk can materialize if the executive committee makes board-level decisions that prove unpopular with the full board. Such a development can create real dissension in the board.

Yet another risk associated with the use of an executive committee relates to authorizing the executive committee to make decisions that should really be approved by the full board. A classic example of this risk occurs when the executive committee is authorized to evaluate or determine the compensation of the CEO. For reasons that are further addressed in Chapter 5, it is always a good idea for the full board to be fully aware of and to approve the CEO's compensation package.

Finally, if an executive committee is utilized and authorized to take action on behalf of the full board, the organization should verify with its legal counsel that the actions authorized are permitted under state law. The laws of most states provide that only the full board, and not a committee, may take certain significant actions.

Applying a "zero-based" approach

Many boards do not need committees of any type. Depending on the competency of management and the nature and scope of the organization's activities, a board may be able to operate perfectly well with no committees. Nonprofit organizations should take a "zero-based" approach to establishing committees – that is, starting with the premise that no board committees are needed and establishing committees only where the need is clearly identified and justified.

In some cases, a specific type of committee may be required by state law. (For example, the laws of California and a few other states require an audit committee for certain types of nonprofit organizations of a certain size.)

Standing vs. ad hoc committees

A board committee is either a standing committee or an ad hoc (temporary, as needed) committee. Ad hoc committees can be very useful to assist the board in evaluating a proposed strategy or policy issue that involves significant detail. Rather than attempt to have the entire board address the matter in detail, with drafts and redrafts, the board may create an ad hoc committee to perform the detailed work and provide a recommendation to the full board. If the board creates an ad hoc committee for such a purpose, the committee should have a clear charter and should be disbanded when its work is complete.

Using risk as the criterion for standing committees

The primary basis for determining the need for a <u>standing</u> committee should be risk-related. In other words, a standing committee may be useful for any area of board oversight that is subject to extraordinary risk, requiring extraordinary attention. In applying a risk-based approach to committee structure, the board's initial tendency may be to identify specific oversight areas such as finance or human resources (HR) that it believes carry such risk, thereby warranting a standing committee's attention. If the organization does, indeed, have a particularly high risk area of operations that warrants the regular attention of a board committee, it should have one. I recommend, however, that the board take a more holistic view of the organization's activities and risks in making such a determination. In doing so, the board may determine that a single "risk management" committee may be just the ticket in lieu of individual board committees each addressing specific areas of risk. A risk management committee of the board may be chartered with the responsibility of overseeing the organization's identification of *all* types of risk, the assessment of risk, and the mitigation of risk. A holistic approach of this type will permit the board to address the organization's entire operating environment and will reduce the risk of blind spots in the board's oversight activities.

Individual board committees can tend to delve into micromanagement of operational matters which are really the responsibility of management. An overall risk management committee may have a lesser tendency to micromanage, given the scope of its charter, and should be able to focus more on strategy and policy issues that are proper matters for board consideration. Chapter 4 addresses the board's role with respect to risk management in more detail.

Executive Recap

- The board should have a conceptual framework for determining if and when board committees are needed.

- A board committee is not an operations group – its activities should be limited to addressing strategy, oversight, and policy issues.

- Every board committee should have a very clear charter.

- An executive committee, if utilized, warrants special consideration.

- Organizations should take a zero-based approach to establishing board committees.

- Ad hoc committees may be used to perform detailed work and provide recommendations to the full board.

- Risk should be the primary criterion for establishing standing committees.

- Use of a single risk management committee in lieu of multiple standing committees may be wise.

4
The Board's Role in Risk Management

A key area of responsibility for the board is to ensure that the organization maintains an adequate approach to risk management in carrying out its programs. While the actual conduct of risk management activities is the responsibility of management under the authority of the CEO, the board should evaluate the organization's risk management strategy since the board has ultimate responsibility for oversight.

An effective risk management plan is a holistic one – one that addresses risk in all aspects of the organization's activities. The risk management plan should also be proactive rather than reactive – identifying risks before they become liabilities and taking appropriate steps to mitigate them.

As described in the preceding chapter, the board may wish to establish a standing committee to oversee the organization's risk management strategy and to provide reports and recommendations to the full board.

The board or risk management committee should work with the CEO to ensure that:

- Risks are identified and assessed as to likelihood of occurrence and severity;

- Risks are prioritized;

- Management has determined the extent to which identified risks have been mitigated; and

- Appropriate steps are taken to reduce identified risks to acceptable levels.

Reducing risk by implementing preventive measures is, of course, different from insuring against such risks. In addition to overseeing the adequacy of risk mitigation, the board should ensure that the organization maintains adequate insurance coverage with respect to applicable risk areas.

Areas of risk to consider

In addressing the organization's overall risks, some key risk areas that warrant attention include, but are not limited to:

- Corporate structure (e.g., whether the organization's activities and assets should all be in one legal entity or perhaps separated to insulate from excessive liability);

- Governing documents (e.g., whether the articles of incorporation and bylaws contain all appropriate provisions and whether the organization's actual governance practices conform to the governing documents);

- Policies and policy manuals (should be addressed for the same reasons that apply to the governing documents);

- Tax-exempt status and compliance;

- Financial condition and financial controls;

- Adequacy of insurance coverage;

- Human resources (personnel);

- Child molestation (for organizations that serve children, as further described below);

- Key operational areas;

- Public relations;

- Physical safety; and

- Leadership succession.

Child molestation risk

For organizations that serve children, child molestation risk warrants special attention due to the severity of the damages that can occur. In recent years, an increasing number of high-liability claims have been made against nonprofit organizations that serve children due to actual or alleged child molestation. Claims of that type can be devastating not only to the victims but also to an organization and its leadership, both reputationally and financially. Multiple Catholic dioceses in the United States have filed for bankruptcy protection in connection with child molestation claims, and many other types of organizations have experienced major claims. The board of a nonprofit organization serving children should carefully evaluate the nature of the risks as well as prevention strategies and insurance coverage maintained by the organization. A variety of very good published resources are available on this topic.

Board members are not expected to be experts in the various risk areas listed above. Rather, the board should ensure that all relevant risk areas are adequately addressed by management under the leadership of the CEO. The organization may engage experts in various disciplines (legal counsel, tax advisors, insurance agents, physical safety experts, etc.) to assist in addressing each area as needed.

Insurance coverage

One significant aspect of risk management includes ensuring that the organization has adequate insurance coverage for its significant risks. The evaluation of insurance coverage should include consultation with both legal counsel and highly experienced insurance agents. Specific coverage types to evaluate should include, but not be limited to:

- Property and casualty (for fire, theft, flood, vandalism, etc.);

- Employee theft;

- General liability;

- Sexual misconduct (including child molestation for organizations that serve children);

- Director and officer liability (see Chapter 7);

- Employment practices (for claims of discrimination, wrongful termination, sexual harassment, and other such matters related to employment practices);

- Fiduciary liability (for claims by employees related to the administration of employee benefit plans, particularly retirement plans); and

- "Key man" life or disability (for financial remuneration to the organization in the event of the death or disability of a key leader – useful where the organization could be adversely affected financially in the event of such an occurrence).

Additional resources for addressing risk management

Some additional sources of information that may be helpful to organizations addressing overall risk management include:

Nonprofit Risk Management Center
(www.nonprofitrisk.org)

Public Entity Risk Institute
(www.riskinstitute.org)

ChurchSafety.com
(www.churchsafety.com)

Executive Recap

- An effective risk management plan is a holistic one.

- The board or risk management committee should work with the CEO to ensure that risks are identified, assessed, prioritized, and adequately mitigated.

- Organizations that serve children should pay special attention to the risk of child molestation.

- The organization should engage experts in various disciplines to assist as needed.

- Adequate insurance coverage is a critical element of risk management.

5
The Board's Role in Financial Matters

In order to ensure sustainability and viability for the organization, the board must maintain appropriate oversight over its financial affairs. The nature, complexity, and scope of the organization's programs and activities will dictate the manner in which the board exercises such oversight. The board may carry out this duty directly or utilize a committee to do so, such as a finance committee. (See Chapter 3 for a discussion of the utilization of committees.)

Whether carried out directly or via committee, the board's financial oversight should extend to the following areas:

- Ensuring that the organization's financial condition is sound and that it has the financial capacity to conduct its programs and activities as intended;

- Adopting and monitoring compliance with appropriate financial policies in conformity with the organization's governing documents;

- Approving and monitoring compliance with the organization's operating budget and capital expenditures budget for each fiscal year;

- Establishing and carefully monitoring compliance with a well-drafted conflicts-of-interest policy (such as the model policy published by the IRS on its website at www.irs.gov) to address transactions with related parties in a manner that represents good governance and compliance with federal tax law (see Chapter 1 for a discussion of conflicts of interest);

- Ensuring that the organization has proper and adequate internal controls over financial operations and activities;

- Ensuring that an independent audit of the organization's financial statements is conducted annually (if the organization's size warrants it) by a CPA firm highly experienced in serving nonprofit organizations and addressing any risk issues raised by the audit firm in connection with the audits;

- Ensuring that the organization's auditors or tax counsel are proactively addressing tax compliance matters and reporting their findings to the board or its designated committee; and

- Properly approving the CEO's compensation package (including all benefits) following federal tax guidelines under the advice of good tax counsel and documenting the board's basis for determining that the compensation is not excessive.

Some thoughts on budgeting

In order to ensure that an organization has adequate financial capacity to carry out its programs and activities, the board must ensure that the organization's financial plan is sound. Sound financial management includes development and approval of a responsible operating budget. Many nonprofit organizations operate under the belief that there is something improper about generating a positive bottom line – that is, a surplus of revenues over expenses. In fact, in many organizations, a desirable budget is a "balanced budget." While operating a balanced budget may sound like an admirable goal, it simply means that the organization expects to incur expenses equal to its revenues, with no room for error. The term "balanced budget" sounds attractive because we would all give our right arms to see our government operate with a balanced budget! But that is no way to improve an organization's financial condition. What's more, since a balanced budget plan leaves no room for error, an unexpected dip in revenues can cause immediate financial stress for an organization and its leaders.

A better approach to budgeting involves determining the organization's desired financial condition (liquidity, reserves, debt levels, etc.) and the desired timetable for achieving it. With a long-term plan for improving financial condition, the organization can develop operating budgets that not only provide for carrying out the organization's mission but also contemplate surpluses to contribute toward the desired financial condition. An organization that has not operated following such a plan may need to reduce program or other expenses in order to implement a strategy of producing responsible budget surpluses.

Engagement of a CPA firm

An organization with $2 million or more in revenues should have an annual audit of its financial statements as part of maintaining financial integrity. Some states, federal funding agencies, and other grant funders require audits at lower revenue levels. In carrying out its oversight responsibilities with respect to financial matters, one highly effective strategy is to maintain a good, proactive relationship with a CPA firm highly experienced in serving nonprofit organizations both in accounting and tax-related matters. A firm with such experience can perform the audit of the organization's financial statements and in so doing, identify many of the risks and vulnerabilities that affect nonprofit organizations. A highly robust approach to auditing the financial statements and reporting findings to the board can identify significant weaknesses, vulnerabilities, deficiencies, or opportunities that may exist in every one of the key financial oversight areas enumerated above. Nonprofit boards (and even their finance committees) rarely have the capacity in time, expertise, or availability to make such assessments themselves. Engaging an audit firm that does not have such experience or does not apply a highly robust approach to the audit process may result in an audit that produces adequately prepared financial statements but a lost opportunity to identify key risk or compliance issues that warrant the attention of the board.

Avoiding financial scandals

The nonprofit sector has been plagued with a number of high-profile national and local financial scandals over the past few decades. A financial scandal often ravages the reputation of the organization's board and management, and adversely affects giving by the organization's donors. High-profile scandals reported in the media are often followed by IRS examinations, which can result in significant penalties and fines against an organization's leaders where abuse is present. Occasionally, such examinations result in criminal prosecution.

Virtually all of the financial scandals in U.S. nonprofit organizations have related to actual or alleged abuses in executive compensation, executive perks, lavish or extravagant expenditures, business transactions with related parties, or the manner in which donor-restricted gifts are spent.

So, what are some effective, but simple safeguards that can be put in place by nonprofit boards to ensure that they don't fall victim to scandals in these areas? For starters, the entire board should be fully aware of the entire compensation package (including benefits and perks) for the organization's CEO and any family members of the CEO. The board should also take steps to ensure that the total compensation is reasonable as compared to what similar organizations pay similarly qualified people to perform similar duties. The board can do the comparability analysis itself or through a board-authorized committee, such as a compensation committee. (See Chapter 3 for a discussion of the use of committees.) If the board utilizes a committee for this purpose, the entire board should be fully aware of the entire compensation package. Under the advice of good tax counsel, the board can follow steps to avail itself of a "rebuttable presumption" under federal tax law that the compensation package is reasonable. Paying excessive compensation to a nonprofit executive is a violation of federal tax law.

Similarly, the board can utilize a well-written conflicts-of-interest policy to address related party transactions as described in Chapter 1. In adopting and applying such a policy, the board should also apply good common sense.

While the organization may get the best price for office supplies from the CEO's brother's company, buying $3 million of supplies from that company may not appear to be highly ethical, and may result in negative media attention as described subsequently in this chapter.

The board should also have a process in place to ensure that it would be notified if the organization were to incur expenditures for travel, meals, hospitality, or other similar activities that could possibly be considered by others to be lavish or extravagant. While a policy can be helpful in this area, simple and effective communication and oversight of expenditures in this area can be helpful as well.

Further, nonprofit boards should have appropriate oversight measures in place to ensure that donor-restricted gifts are spent in a manner that conforms to donor expectations. Basic policies and expenditure oversight can accomplish this objective. A very helpful resource in this area is the book *Donor-Restricted Gifts Simplified* by Dan Busby, available at www.ecfa.org or on www.amazon.com. The organization's auditing firm should also be a source of helpful insights.

Additionally, requiring that every board meeting include standing agenda items to discuss "sensitive" topics can help dramatically reduce risk in these areas. For example, a standing agenda item may be to receive a report of expenditures or activities in which the organization's management has engaged that could possibly be construed by others to be lavish, extravagant, or providing some personal benefit.

Watch out for media spin!

You have undoubtedly heard the expression, "No good deed goes unpunished." There is probably no setting where that cynical axiom is truer than with nonprofit organizations. An organization can feed a thousand children in a poverty-stricken community, and a newspaper may report the fact that adults were excluded or that several kids somehow missed out. An organization can raise a million dollars for disease research at a fancy gala, and the resulting news story may focus on the ice carving at the event that cost $5,000.

An organization can engage in an activity or business transaction that makes economic sense for the organization, but it may be reported by the media in a manner that makes it sound like abuse. For example, if a nonprofit organization's board member sells an office building to the organization for 20% less than its appraised value (completely in compliance with the organization's conflicts-of-interest policy and federal tax law), the news media may ignore the discount element of the transaction and simply report that the organization "paid $2 million to one of its board members in an insider real estate deal."

I advise clients to use the "front-page test" as a filter for deciding whether to enter into any transaction that could have a "negative spin" possibility. That is, the board should ask the question, "Could this transaction or decision be reported by the media in a way that could cause embarrassment or damage to the organization or its leaders?" If the answer is "yes," it may be best to avoid the proposed action.

Executive Recap

- The board must maintain appropriate oversight over the organization's financial affairs – either directly or through a committee.

- Financial oversight should extend to the areas enumerated in this chapter.

- A "balanced budget" is probably not an ideal financial operating plan.

- The organization should determine its desired financial condition and use budgeting as a strategy to achieve it.

- Engaging a CPA firm highly experienced in serving nonprofits with respect to both accounting and tax matters is a highly effective strategy to facilitate sound financial management.

- An organization may avoid financial scandals of the types that have been reported in the media by following a few common-sense practices.

- The organization's leaders should watch out for media spin related to its activities, using the "front-page test" to determine whether to take certain actions.

6
Governing and Policy Documents

While boards have ultimate authority and responsibility for the oversight of their organization, well-governed organizations will operate pursuant to a hierarchy of governing and policy documents. Such documents establish the parameters within which the organization, its board, and its leadership are to operate and are indispensable in establishing stability.

The legal hierarchy of governing and policy documents is not a matter of opinion or debate, but rather a matter of law. If a conflict exists between two or more documents in the hierarchy, the higher-level document trumps the others.

The hierarchy of documents is as follows:

- State law

- Federal tax law

- Articles of incorporation

- Bylaws

- Policies (adopted by the board)

- Procedures (adopted by management)

State law

As described in Chapter 1, the laws of the state in which the organization was incorporated establish the ultimate legal authority within which the organization must operate. Every state has such laws. Portions of state nonprofit corporation law apply regardless of the provisions in the organization's articles of incorporation or bylaws. For example, Florida Statutes Section 617.0833 prohibits loans by a Florida nonprofit corporation to its officers, directors, and certain other related parties, regardless of whether the organization's articles of incorporation or bylaws permit such loans.

Other portions of state nonprofit corporation law provide authority regarding certain matters, but defer to the organization's articles of incorporation or bylaws if they contain conflicting provisions. For example, Section 108.15(b) of the Illinois General Not For Profit Corporation Act states, "The act of the majority of the directors present at a meeting at which a quorum is present shall be the act of the board of directors, unless the act of a greater number is required by the articles of incorporation or the bylaws."

Since each state has unique laws covering employment, charitable solicitation, and other matters, nonprofit corporations incorporated in one state but operating in one or more other states should consult their legal counsel to determine which state laws apply or control.

Federal tax law

Nonprofit organizations obtain their federal tax-exempt status through federal tax law, which dictates various criteria for obtaining and maintaining tax-exempt status. Tax-exempt organizations must take care to ensure compliance with applicable federal tax law in order to avoid losing their exemption. A detailed analysis of tax law compliance requirements is outside the scope of this book. However, as described in Chapter 5, the board should ensure that the organization has engaged highly experienced and competent tax counsel to proactively assess the organization's compliance with applicable tax laws.

Articles of incorporation

The articles of incorporation (sometimes referred to as the "charter") of a nonprofit corporation is the document that gives legal life to the organization. A corporation is a legal entity created by filing the articles of incorporation with the appropriate state agency. The articles of incorporation are the highest-ranking governing document of the organization. Because the original document is filed with the state, amendments to the articles of incorporation must also be filed with the state. An organization's articles of incorporation and related amendments are public documents.

The articles of incorporation must contain certain minimum provisions under state law – typically the name and initial address of the organization, purpose language, an indication as to whether the organization has members, the names of initial board members, and the like. Additionally, a nonprofit organization that is or plans to be exempt from federal income tax as a charitable, religious, or educational organization described in Section 501(c)(3) of the Internal Revenue Code must include in its articles of incorporation certain provisions limiting the activities of the organization to those permitted for such exempt organizations.

It is permissible for an organization to include in the articles any amount of detail it wishes regarding the organization's governance. However, since all amendments to the articles must be filed with the state agency, it is common practice to make the articles of incorporation rather minimal in content and to include the organization's more detailed governance provisions in the bylaws, which are easier to amend.

A nonprofit organization should consult legal counsel with significant nonprofit experience when drafting its original articles of incorporation or any amendments to them.

Bylaws

The bylaws of an organization typically contain the specific governance provisions of the organization. While some organizations duplicate certain language, such as the organization's purpose, in both the bylaws and the articles of incorporation, doing so raises the risk that the two documents will get out of sync at some point and, for that reason, is not advisable. Typical provisions in an organization's bylaws include, but are not limited to:

- Qualifications of members and process for joining (for organizations that have members);

- Qualifications for board members and terms of office;

- Process for the election and removal of board members and for filling board vacancies;

- Corporate officer titles, duties, responsibilities, election, removal, and terms of office;

- Information about the conduct of meetings, including quorum requirements and voting requirements (which may include supermajority voting requirements for certain matters);

- Indemnification of board members and officers with respect to liability stemming from the performance of their duties for the organization;

- The organization's fiscal year; and

- Requirements for amendment of the articles of incorporation and bylaws.

The organization should consult legal counsel with significant nonprofit experience for the drafting or amendment of its bylaws.

Policies

The nomenclature used in the area of "policies" varies dramatically in practice, so let's address that from the outset. The term "policies" can mean any number of things, including board resolutions, board-approved policy documents, management-approved documents, and more. Some distinguish between "board policies" and "management policies."

I prefer to distinguish between the guiding documents approved by the board and those approved by management by referring to board-approved documents as "policies" and management-approved documents as "procedures." No clear right or wrong approach to nomenclature exists, but it is essential to distinguish between the two in some clear and appropriate manner.

For example, the board of a nonprofit adoption agency may establish a policy requiring prospective parents to complete a criminal background check and to have no record of felonies or violent crimes. The CEO may establish a procedure further clarifying the policy by requiring that the background check be national in scope and defining the specific types of criminal violations that are not acceptable for prospective parents. It is important that the distinction be made between the board's policy and the CEO's procedure so that, if the CEO wants to modify the list of unacceptable crimes, it is clear that he/she may do so without board approval, so long as the new procedure still complies with the board's policy.

The board is responsible for adopting and maintaining such policies as it believes are necessary and appropriate to establish parameters for the orderly operation of the organization. It is not necessary or advisable for the board's policies to replicate provisions that are included in the articles of incorporation or the bylaws, since doing so raises the risk that the documents will get out of sync at some point. The board should adopt only those policies that are truly necessary for the legal and orderly operation of the organization.

Procedures

Management-adopted procedures represent guidance for the organization's staff under the leadership of the CEO. Procedures adopted by management should not conflict with board-approved policies or the organization's governing documents (articles of incorporation and bylaws). In fact, such procedures should typically address specific aspects of implementing the organization's board-approved policies or governing documents.

The importance of legal counsel

The board should ensure that legal counsel with significant nonprofit experience reviews all of the organization's governing and policy documents and advises the board regarding their propriety. Such a review should be conducted periodically to address changes that are made in the documents over time as well as changes that occur in the legal environment.

Hooey Alert!

Other than the requirements of state law and federal tax law for nonprofit organizations to include certain provisions in the articles of incorporation and bylaws as a condition for incorporation or tax exemption, there are rarely other legal requirements for nonprofit organizations to have specific board-approved policies. Much misinformation (hooey) is communicated in this area of board governance and much confusion exists as a result. The two primary sources of hooey in this area are:

- Those who state or imply that the *Sarbanes-Oxley Act,* which applies to publicly-traded companies, somehow applies in a similar fashion to nonprofit organizations; and

- The IRS.

Sarbanes-Oxley

Some of the confusion stems from the invalid assertion or implication in some nonprofit publications or other media that the *Sarbanes-Oxley Act* passed by Congress to govern the affairs of publicly-traded companies somehow applies to nonprofit organizations in the same manner. It has not and it does not! Notwithstanding that fact, the nonprofit community is still rife with publications and presentations stating or implying otherwise. A simple Google search of the term "nonprofit" together with "Sarbanes-Oxley" will reap a mother lode of "resources" on the topic, along with litanies of recommendations regarding various policies that nonprofits "should" adopt.

It is true that two provisions of *Sarbanes-Oxley* apply to nonprofits – but the reason they do is because they apply to everyone in America! Those two provisions relate to:

1. Retaliating against a "whistleblower" – someone who reports illegal activity, and

2. Destroying, altering, or falsifying documents that are the subject of a federal proceeding.

Even with respect to these two provisions of the *Sarbanes-Oxley Act*, there is no requirement that nonprofits have specific policies in place. The Act simply makes it a federal crime to violate the whistleblower and record retention provisions of the law.

The IRS and policy requirements

The IRS is another primary source of rampant confusion regarding policy requirements for nonprofit organizations. After concluding that poor board governance was at the root of virtually all high-profile financial scandals that arose in the nonprofit sector in the past several decades, the IRS decided in the mid-2000s that nonprofit organizations should be pressured into adopting certain governance policies and practices.

In 2008, the IRS radically modified the annual federal information form that most nonprofits file (Form 990) to include numerous questions about whether the filing organization has adopted a variety of policies or practices related to its governance. The IRS added such questions to the form notwithstanding the fact that federal tax law contains no requirements for an organization to adopt

42

such policies or practices as a condition of maintaining tax-exempt status.

As a result, a nonprofit organization filing Form 990 must now answer questions in this publicly-disseminated form such as:

- The number of the organization's board members who are "independent" (the IRS arbitrarily devised its own definition of independence for this purpose);

- Whether the organization has a conflicts-of-interest policy governing transactions between the organization and its insiders;

- Whether the organization has a whistleblower policy;

- Whether the organization has a record retention policy;

- Whether the organization's board reviews the Form 990 before it is filed with the IRS;

- Whether the organization follows highly-specific procedures in establishing executive compensation;

- Whether the organization has a policy covering executive expense reimbursements; and

- Whether the organization has a gift acceptance policy.

By adding such questions to the Form 990, the IRS knowingly created an environment of pressure for nonprofit organizations to adopt policies and practices that would allow them to answer "Yes!" Answering "yes" helps organizations avoid appearing to be recalcitrant. Many advisors in the nonprofit sector, myself included, believe that "no" answers to such questions raise the risk of an IRS audit.

In late 2009, the IRS announced that it would have its examination agents ask numerous questions about an organization's governance practices in every examination of nonprofit organizations for a period of time. Among the numerous issues the agents are to address is the attendance record of individual board members at board meetings! The IRS's apparent reason for obtaining such information during examinations is to document what it believes is the correlation between poor board governance and noncompliance with federal tax law.

As a result of the IRS's pressure, most large and respected nonprofit organizations have adopted policies and practices of the types addressed in the Form 990. Such policies, if drafted carefully in a manner that is appropriate for the organization, can be helpful, but they are not a requirement for tax exemption.

Familiarity and compliance with governing and policy documents

Every board member should read and be familiar with the organization's articles of incorporation, bylaws, and board-approved policies. Those documents provide the framework within which the board and management are to conduct their business. The board should ensure that the organization operates in compliance with its governing and policy documents. Failure to do so will likely result in a disorderly operating environment and may create significant legal problems for the organization and its leaders.

Executive Recap

- Well-governed organizations operate pursuant to a hierarchy of governing and policy documents with which each board member should be familiar.

- If a conflict exists between documents in the hierarchy, the higher-level document trumps.

- It is essential to distinguish between board-approved policies and management-approved procedures.

- The board should ensure that highly competent legal counsel reviews all of the organization's governing and policy documents.

- The *Sarbanes-Oxley Act* does not require nonprofit organizations to adopt any specific policies.

- The IRS has intimidated nonprofit organizations into adopting various governance policies that are not required by law.

- The IRS has begun evaluating board governance practices in connection with its examinations of nonprofit organizations.

7

The Liability of Board Members

The outset of this chapter on board member liability presents an ideal opportunity to make the case for nonprofit boards maintaining an appropriate, proactive relationship with general legal counsel. Far too often, nonprofit organizations consult legal counsel only on a reactive basis, and only when an issue has become a legal problem. The board of a nonprofit organization should select general legal counsel to advise and represent it in its decision-making. The attorney or firm selected should have an excellent reputation in the community as well as significant experience serving nonprofit organizations.

As mentioned in Chapter 6, legal counsel should advise the board on changes to the organization's governing and policy documents. Additionally, the organization should ask counsel to review and assist in the drafting of all significant contractual agreements contemplated by the organization before they are executed.

The board should also ensure that the organization has an appropriate, holistic risk management strategy in place as described in Chapter 4.

By maintaining a proactive relationship with legal counsel and an appropriate risk management strategy, the board can tremendously reduce the risk of unexpected liability for itself or for the organization.

Hooey Alert!

Many urban legends and myths are propagated in nonprofit circles around the idea that nonprofit board members can easily be sued individually and held liable for their actions or inactions if they are not sufficiently careful in carrying out their duties.

It is true, of course, that anyone in America can sue anyone else in America for any reason any time, without regard to the merits of their case. Bearing the costs and possible repercussions of filing a baseless or frivolous lawsuit, however, is quite another matter, which is why such lawsuits are not commonplace.

While it is certainly true that nonprofit organizations face exposure to a variety of risks and potential liability depending on the nature of their activities, it is actually quite rare for board members themselves to be sued in their individual capacities or held liable for damages in connection with their service on nonprofit boards.

Civil immunity

One major reason that nonprofit board members are rarely sued individually is that the laws of many states contain statutory provisions stating that volunteer board members (and often, other volunteers) of nonprofit organizations may not be held personally liable in connection with carrying out their duties in good faith. Obviously, a statutory "shield" of this type is a powerful force, making it virtually futile to attempt to hold volunteer board members liable for their actions or inactions.

The importance of volunteering vs. being compensated

A critical element of civil immunity laws is that they often apply only if the nonprofit board members are uncompensated. Very few nonprofit organizations compensate their board members for their service, as volunteer board service represents a charitable act in and of itself. For those organizations who would contemplate paying their board members, among the several considerations they should weigh is whether such compensation would cause the board members to lose statutory immunity from liability.

Other ways civil immunity can be lost

Where state laws provide immunity for volunteer board members, such laws sometimes contain provisions stating that nonprofit board members lose their immunity if they engage in certain actions. For example, Florida law prohibits Florida nonprofit corporations from making loans to their officers or directors or to certain parties related to them. The law may be read to imply that violating the loan prohibition causes board members to lose the civil immunity that is otherwise available to them under the law.

Nonprofit boards should have their legal counsel advise them as to whether applicable state laws offer civil immunity for board members or other persons serving the organization. Counsel should also advise the board of any conditions for maintaining such immunity, so that the board may govern itself accordingly.

Indemnification of board members

Notwithstanding the fact that state law may provide some measure of immunity from liability for board members, nonprofit organizations commonly agree to indemnify (cover the cost of claims made against) their board members and officers in connection with carrying out their official duties. Organizations wishing to provide such indemnification typically include language to that effect in the organization's bylaws. As part of legal counsel's review of the bylaws, counsel should specifically address whether the indemnification language adequately and appropriately provides for the desired degree of protection.

Director and officer liability insurance

In addition to the layers of protection described previously in this chapter, nonprofit boards should insist that the organization maintain an insurance policy adequately covering the potential liability of board members in the event they are sued. As we recognized previously, anyone can sue anyone else any time for any reason, regardless of whether the case has merit. When faced with a lawsuit, board members need to know that not only has the organization agreed to indemnify them, but also that adequate funds are available to do so. That is the role of director and officer (D&O) liability insurance. The board should determine the level of coverage (coverage limits) that it considers adequate and select an insurance company (carrier) with a solid reputation and solid financial position. The board's legal counsel should review the insurance policy and advise the board regarding significant exclusions from coverage that may exist in the policy as well as other relevant aspects of the policy. Many persons knowledgeable about the world of nonprofit board service will refuse to serve on a board that does not have adequate D&O coverage (myself included). Given the importance to the board members of such coverage, nonprofit organizations should make it a practice to provide board members with a copy of the D&O policy every year when it is renewed, and the board's calendar should contain a reminder to do so each year.

Executive Recap

- With a combination of acting in good faith, proactively engaging legal counsel, maintaining an appropriate risk management strategy, availing itself of civil immunity provisions that may exist under state law, providing in the bylaws for indemnification by the organization, and maintaining adequate D&O coverage, the nonprofit board should be comfortable with its overall risk level.

- It is actually quite rare for board members themselves to be sued in their individual capacities or held liable for damages in connection with their service on nonprofit boards.

8

Understanding, Evaluating, and Protecting Mission

Every nonprofit organization should have a clear statement describing its mission and/or purpose. Such a statement is commonly referred to as a "mission statement" or "purpose statement." I will not attempt in this book to address the distinction between stating the mission of an organization and stating its purpose. There are lots of folks who are passionate about the distinction between the two. I am not one of them, and I will refer to such a statement as a "mission statement" from here forward. An organization needs to have a mission statement – one that helps its board and leadership know what the organization is about – what it seeks to accomplish. Without a clear mission statement, what does a board use as a reference point to determine whether the organization should pursue a particular strategic initiative or not? Or, how does a board determine whether the activities an organization is conducting are "on mission" or not?

The breadth or narrowness of the mission statement should be the determinative factor regarding the nature and scope of the organization's work. For this reason, an appropriate degree of specificity is helpful. For example, an organization whose calling is to make a difference in the lives of young people in the community could draft its mission statement in a variety of ways.

An example of a relatively broad mission statement would be:

> *Light & Hope exists to make a positive difference in the lives of young people in the Central Heights area.*

While the mission statement above does contain some geographic specificity, the terms "make a positive difference" and "young people" are relatively broad and could mean any number of things.

An example of a more specifically worded mission statement would be:

> *Light & Hope exists to make a positive difference in the lives of children up to age seventeen in the Central Heights area by offering excellent after-school activities focused on educational support, character-building, healthy recreation, and nutrition.*

This more specific mission statement provides a much greater degree of clarity to the organization's leadership regarding the nature and scope of its activities.

The board's ownership of the mission

The board must "own" the organization's mission, meaning that it must understand it, believe in it, promote it, and protect it. If the mission statement needs to be modified in order for it to be sufficiently clear or to more closely match the organization's calling, the board should modify it accordingly. Once the mission of the organization is defined clearly, every board member must believe in it and fully support it. Individuals who are not able to do so should not serve on the board, as they would represent a threat to the organization and its mission.

Promoting the mission means ensuring that the organization carries out effective programs and activities that accomplish the mission. A key board responsibility is to evaluate the effectiveness with which the mission is being carried out and to hold the CEO or top management official accountable.

Preventing "mission drift" or "mission creep"

Protecting the mission of the organization means not permitting the organization or its leadership to pursue programs or activities that are outside the scope of the organization's mission. Conducting non-mission programs or activities is sometimes referred to as "mission drift" or "mission creep." An organization's management or board may have great ideas for very worthy initiatives that are outside the organization's mission. For example, the management of Light & Hope (the fictional organization referred to previously in this chapter) might have an idea to teach literacy to adults in the Central Heights area. While teaching adult literacy is unquestionably a noble activity, it does not fit within the stated mission of the organization. Nonprofit organizations have limited resources that must be allocated among their various programs and activities. Using those limited resources to conduct off-mission activities will adversely affect the effectiveness of the organization's key mission-based activities. Protecting the mission of the organization requires discipline and focus, and can at times be unpleasant. When the board advises management that it does not approve of or support the adult literacy program proposed by management, hard feelings can ensue depending on the dynamics of the people and the circumstances. A board that regularly discusses and proactively reminds itself and management of the need to stay on-mission is much less likely to encounter such bumps in the road.

The difference between preventing "mission drift" or "mission creep" and preserving the *original* mission

Many older nonprofit organizations started out with a specific mission or purpose that would be virtually unrecognizable in the organization today. The YMCA, for example, was originally founded in 1844 in industrialized London by 22-year-old George Williams. According to the Y, Mr. Williams "joined 11 friends to organize the first Young Men's Christian Association (YMCA), a refuge of Bible study and prayer for young men seeking escape from the hazards of life on the streets." Few people today would associate the Y's programs and activities primarily with either "young men" or "Bible study and prayer."

One very important question for a nonprofit board is the extent to which it should strive to preserve its *original* mission – that is, the mission assigned to the organization by its founders. Over time, cultural contexts change, and boards are sometimes faced with decisions about whether to modify the *original* mission. In some cases, the answer may be clear. For example, an organization formed to help people in the United States suffering from polio would largely be irrelevant today, thanks to the virtual eradication of the disease. In other cases, the decision may be more difficult. An organization established to help reduce poverty in a community may watch as the community's economy improves while a neighboring area deteriorates. Should the organization modify its mission to serve surrounding areas, or should it continue to focus on the few remaining poverty victims in its community? Unless the founders were clear in expressing their original intentions about such possibilities, the board must make such a decision based on what it believes is best.

Boards that wish to preserve an organization's *original* mission should take affirmative steps to do so while the board is composed of people who support the idea. Otherwise, future boards may hijack the organization's mission and divert it in ways that its founders never could have imagined. There are a variety of ways to reduce the risk of future boards changing the organization's mission, and legal counsel can advise the board regarding its options.

Executive Recap

- Every nonprofit organization should have a clear statement describing its mission or purpose.

- The board must "own" the organization's mission.

- A key responsibility of the board is to evaluate the effectiveness with which the mission is being carried out and to hold the CEO accountable.

- Protecting the mission of the organization requires discipline and focus, and can at times be unpleasant.

- Boards that wish to preserve an organization's *original* mission should take affirmative steps to do so while the board is composed of members who support the idea.

9
Board Meeting Dynamics

Every nonprofit board has its own culture, which invariably affects the dynamics of its meetings. Some organizations take a quite formal approach to conducting board meetings while others are rather casual. As long as the proper business of the board is carried out in a manner that conforms to the organization's governing and policy documents, the degree of formality with which the meetings are conducted is of little relevance.

All boards, however, can benefit from considering certain principles and practices that aid in maintaining more effective boardmanship and more efficient, orderly meetings.

Parliamentary procedure

Most boards purport to follow some version of parliamentary procedure, often citing Robert's Rules of Order as the source of authority. In reality, however, very few organizations follow Robert's Rules closely. For example, Robert's Rules would generally require that a motion be made and seconded before discussion may ensue for a proposed board action. Most boards do exactly the opposite. They engage in extensive discussion on a proposal followed by a motion, second and vote on the matter. The degree to which an organization attempts to follow parliamentary procedure is up to the organization's board. Most organizations operate quite well using a relaxed approach to parliamentary procedure. At times when a particular issue becomes complex or there are multiple views on a proposed action, adherence to parliamentary procedure may be necessary to maintain order. A number of good publications are available on the topic of parliamentary procedure, including some that are modernized and summarized.

Attendance

Board members should plan to attend every board meeting of the organization. Service on the board requires commitment to an appropriate level of engagement and involvement, and meeting attendance is an essential element of responsible involvement. An individual who cannot attend meetings regularly should not agree to serve on the board, as the organization will not have the full benefit of his/her expertise in decision-making. Many nonprofit boards have provisions in their bylaws or board polices requiring a minimum level of attendance and requiring that board members who miss meetings frequently be removed from their position.

Preparation for board meetings

The chair and CEO of a well-governed nonprofit organization will send all board members a package of information relevant to each upcoming board meeting at least seven to ten days prior to the meeting. The information package should include a copy of the agenda, information about the main action items to be considered, copies of the CEO's report, and any other departmental reports or other background information that will help board members be better prepared for the discussions. Board members should take time to read the information carefully prior to the meeting so that the meeting discussions do not include wasting time with background information. Failure to prepare for board meetings drags down the efficiency of the meeting and is frustrating to the board members who come prepared.

The role of the chair

The board chair (chairman, chairwoman, chairperson) has the single most important role in defining the dynamics of a board meeting. Chairs that are highly effective can lead an organization's board to excellence while ineffective chairs can unwittingly be the cause of significant dysfunction in the board room. The chair moderates the meeting and should establish a courteous tone that commands order and respect. A key task of the chair is to set the agenda for the meeting in cooperation with the CEO. The agenda should be well-planned and all expected matters that are to be proposed to the board for action should be clearly identified and articulated in writing prior to the meeting. For example, rather than expecting the CEO to informally propose a new policy at the board meeting, the proposed policy language should be completely drafted prior to the meeting, along with an indication of the exact location in the board policy manual where the new policy will be inserted. A proposed board resolution adopting the new policy should be drafted as well and presented at the meeting. Such preplanning makes the board's consideration of the matter much more efficient and eliminates the need for board members to create detailed motions on the fly.

The chair should also insist on sticking to the agenda and limiting discussion and debate to matters that are germane to the proposal or motion under consideration. Massive amounts of time can be wasted in board meetings when board members are permitted to ramble or initiate irrelevant discussions.

The chair should also see to it that the views of all interested board members are heard with respect to significant matters under consideration. If discussion is being dominated by a small number of board members, the chair should ask for other views on the matter. The chair should ask individuals by name to share their thoughts when they have not been vocal on a significant topic.

The chair must be respectful of the views of all board members, even when they are different from his. The chair must also demand that board members be respectful of the views of each other. Passionate debate about an issue is actually quite healthy, so long as the parties debating maintain civility and a healthy respect for each other. I have sometimes found myself debating passionately for a particular viewpoint, only to be persuaded to support the opposing view after carefully listening to the counterarguments. Nonprofit boards are at their absolute best when all board members are engaged and all board members seek the result that is best for the organization, regardless of whose idea it is. Some of my favorite memories of board meetings are those that involved "heated debate" followed by good-natured ribbing and laughter after the vote.

Additionally, board members should remember that regardless of whether there was agreement on an issue before the vote, once the board has voted an on issue, the board members must be unified in supporting the actions and policies of the board. Any board member who is unable to do so should resign from the board.

Engaging in the "tough" discussions

In order to properly carry out their responsibilities, board members must sometimes engage in difficult discussions in the board room. They must sometimes ask difficult questions that can make others in the room uncomfortable. For example, if a board member has reason to suspect that a transaction under consideration may violate the organization's conflicts-of-interest policy, he or she should speak up and ask about it during deliberations. Similarly, if a board member has concerns about the integrity of fundraising materials being disseminated by the organization, he or she should address the issue at the proper time. Occasions when board members have such concerns are often the forks in the road that determine whether an organization takes the ethical high road or the low road in its decision-making. There is no room for ignoring issues that require board attention no matter how difficult, uncomfortable, or contentious they may be.

Certain strategies can reduce the discomfort level in the board room regarding such issues. An organization with a healthy culture of regularly and proactively asking tough questions will have much less difficulty doing so. Another helpful strategy is to create standing agenda items that are automatically placed on the agenda for board or committee consideration without any board member having to bring them up. Such standing agenda items could include, for example:

- Annual consideration of the reasonableness of the CEO's compensation package;

- Review of the CEO's expenses for travel, meals, and hospitality;

- Discussion of details of any related party transaction; or

- Reports from management of any expenses incurred by the organization that may cause the organization to be vulnerable to criticism or that may be considered by some to be lavish or extravagant.

By identifying the types of issues that can be uncomfortable and making them standing agenda items, board members can engage in the related discussions more comfortably, maintain a healthy, open culture, and reduce the organization's risk.

Keeping minutes

Someone in the meeting – typically the corporate secretary or his/her designee – is responsible for keeping the official minutes of the meeting. Minutes are the official, legal records of board actions that occur during board meetings. The board should obtain advice from the organization's legal counsel regarding the proper content and format of the minutes. Most attorneys suggest that details be kept to a minimum. The minutes should ordinarily include the following information:

- Date and time the meeting started;

- List of board members present and absent;

- List of guests present;

- Call to order;

- Confirmation that a quorum is present;

- A statement reflecting any report that is made to the board (e.g., the CEO's report), including a general description of the subject and conclusions, but not the details of the report;

- For each motion presented to the board for consideration, a record of:

  o the precise wording of the motion,

  o who made the motion,

  o who seconded the motion (if a second was required),

  o the fact that there was discussion on the matter (if true), including the general nature of the discussion, but not details of the discussion, and

  o whether the motion passed or failed;

- Reference to any documents that are made part of the minutes by virtue of the passing of a motion or other board action; and

- Time the meeting adjourned.

Confidentiality

The board should maintain and enforce a policy of confidentiality regarding matters coming to its attention and board members should assume that *everything* is confidential. Confidentiality is a serious matter, and failure to observe it can have serious consequences. Some matters of discussion are obviously sensitive in nature and confidentiality with respect to such matters usually comes naturally to most board members. Examples would include discussions about the CEO's performance, the health of a key employee, and threatened litigation, to name a few. An issue does not have to seem sensitive, however, to warrant confidentiality. There are very good reasons for treating *all* matters discussed as being confidential. For example, suppose the board discusses possible budget cuts in one of its programs. Leaks about such a discussion could adversely affect employee morale or donor perceptions and could have other unanticipated consequences. Communications that are made outside the board room related to any board discussion or decision should consist only of official communications by the board's authorized spokesperson. In most cases, that will be the CEO.

Encourage one another

Board meeting discussions and debate can be challenging and draining even when all parties are civil and respectful of each other. Board members should also remember that the proposals brought to them for consideration have often required substantial preparation and consideration by management or other board members who have the organization's best interests at heart. When such proposals are voted down or are criticized during discussion and debate, the effect can be discouraging to those who developed them. Board members can foster a positive environment if they encourage management and their fellow board members by genuinely recognizing the efforts that are put into developing proposals and their positive attributes, whether they are ultimately approved or not.

Few endeavors in life are more rewarding than working together as volunteers in an encouraging environment to make a positive difference in the lives of people. Serving on a nonprofit board is a great privilege. May God bless you as you serve.

Executive Recap

- As long as the proper business of the board is carried out in a manner that conforms to the organization's governing and policy documents, the degree of formality with which the meetings are conducted is of little relevance.

- Board members should plan to attend every board meeting of the organization.

- The board chair has the single most important role in defining the dynamics of a board meeting.

- There is no room for ignoring issues that require board attention no matter how difficult, uncomfortable, or contentious they may be.

- The board should maintain and enforce a policy of confidentiality regarding matters coming to its attention.

- Board members can foster a positive environment if they encourage management and their fellow board members by genuinely recognizing the efforts that are put into developing proposals and their positive attributes, whether they are ultimately approved or not.

10
Completing the Orientation Process by Providing Organization-Specific Information to Board Members

Your board member orientation process must address two essential components:

- General information about the world of nonprofit board service, and

- Specific information about the unique attributes of your organization.

The Board Member Orientation Process

Step 1

Have board members read Chapters 1-9 of this book. Chapters 1-9 of this book are designed to provide board members with an overview of the general aspects of nonprofit board service.

Step 2

Provide board members with copies of your organization's **Governing, Policy, and Other Important Documents** of the types listed on the following page and ask each board member to review them.

Step 3

Gather the board members for a meeting to talk about the **Discussion Questions** on the following pages as they apply to your organization.

Step 4

Your orientation process is complete!

Governing, Policy, and Other Important Documents

1. Articles of incorporation (current version, as amended)

2. Bylaws (current version, as amended)

3. Mission or purpose statement

4. Charters of all board committees (if applicable)

5. Board-approved policies or policy manuals

6. Director and officer liability insurance policy

7. Most recent audited financial statements of the organization and related report from auditors on significant weaknesses, risks, or compliance matters

8. Most recent Form 990 filed with the Internal Revenue Service (if applicable)

9. Most recent annual report (if applicable)

10. A brief history of the organization and current literature describing or promoting the organization's programs and activities

11. Minutes of the most recent board meeting

12. List of current board members and officers

Discussion Questions

(Where appropriate, in lieu of providing a detailed answer below, simply indicate the reference to the applicable provision(s) of the governing or policy documents listed above.)

1. In what state was the organization formed or incorporated?

2. When was the organization formed or incorporated?

3. What is the stated mission of the organization? [*See Chapter 8 for information on this topic.*]

4. Do the organization's current activities conform to its mission statement? [*See Chapter 8 for information on this topic.*]

5. Does the organization operate in conformity with its articles of incorporation, bylaws, and board policies? [*See Chapter 6 for information on this topic.*]

6. Does the organization have voting members who elect the board?

    a. If the organization has voting members:

        i. What other rights and authority do members have?

        ii. Is membership approval required for changes to the articles of incorporation or bylaws?

    b. If the organization does <u>not</u> have voting members:

        i. How is the board elected or appointed?

        ii. Who has authority to amend the articles of incorporation and bylaws?

7. What are the terms of office for board members?

8. Do board members have term limits? If so, what are they?

9. How often and when are board meetings held?

10. How long do board meetings typically last?

11. What do the bylaws require for a quorum in a board meeting?

12. What types of board action (if any) require a supermajority vote (approval by more than a majority) and what percentage of board members must approve each?

a. For actions that require a supermajority vote, does the requirement stipulate that the vote of those approving the matter must comprise: 1) a percentage of board members present, or 2) a percentage of board members holding office at the time?

13. What board committees exist and what are their functions? [*See Chapter 3 for information on this topic.*]

14. What are the expectations of board members between board meetings, other than to prepare for the next meeting by reading the materials provided in advance of the meeting?

15. What are the expectations of board members with respect to fundraising? [*See Chapter 2 for information on this topic.*]

16. What corporate officer positions does the organization have and what are their duties and responsibilities?

17. Does state law provide for immunity from liability for the board members? If yes, what are the conditions for qualifying? (This question may require input from the organization's legal counsel.) [*See Chapter 7 for information on this topic.*]

18. Do the bylaws contain language providing for indemnification of the liability of board members and officers in connection with the performance of their duties? [*See Chapter 7 for information on this topic.*]

19. What is the coverage limit for director and officer (D&O) liability in the organization's D&O insurance policy? [*See Chapter 7 for information on this topic.*]

    a. Is the coverage level considered adequate?

    b. Is the insurance carrier deemed financially solid?

20. What are the major risks faced by the organization in conducting its programs and activities? [*See Chapter 4 for information on this topic.*]

    a. Are such risks adequately mitigated?

    b. If the organization serves children, does it have robust policies and procedures to substantially reduce the risk of child molestation or similar abuse in its programs and activities?

21. Does management believe the insurance coverage maintained by the organization is adequate in all relevant risk areas? [*See Chapter 4 for information on this topic.*]

22. Does the organization enjoy a good reputation in its community and among its constituents and the media?

23. Is the rapport between the board and the CEO good?

24. Does the board refrain from micromanagement and interference in operational matters? [*See Chapter 2 for information on this topic.*]

25. Is the organization in stable financial condition, and does it have the financial capacity to carry out its intended programs and activities? [*See Chapter 5 for information on this topic.*]

26. What is the organization's process for developing and approving budgets? [*See Chapter 5 for information on this topic.*]

27. Is the organization, to the best of management's knowledge and belief, in compliance with all applicable laws and regulations?

28. Is the organization adequately addressing significant weaknesses, risks, compliance issues, or opportunities

reported by its independent auditors (if applicable)? [*See Chapter 5 for information on this topic.*]

29. Does the board have a current conflicts-of-interest policy governing transactions between the organization and its board members, officers, and management, and has the organization obtained guidance from tax counsel that the policy conforms to current federal tax law? [*See Chapters 1 and 5 for information on this topic.*]

    a. Does the organization carefully monitor compliance with the policy?

30. Does the board have a clear policy or practice covering the manner in which compensation of the CEO is established? [*See Chapter 5 for information on this topic.*]

    a. Does the policy or practice involve obtaining comparability data for compensation of persons in similar positions with similar duties in similar organizations, and is that information documented as part of the compensation-setting process?

    b. Is the full board aware of the complete compensation package and benefits provided to the CEO and does the board approve the full package annually?

    c. If members of the CEO's family are employed by the organization, is the board made aware of their compensation and benefits at least annually?

    d. Has the organization obtained guidance from tax counsel that its process for establishing the CEO's compensation meets the guidelines in federal tax law to create a "presumption" that the compensation is reasonable?

31. Does the board have an effective mechanism to monitor for reasonableness the expenses incurred by management for travel, meals, hospitality, and similar activities? [*See Chapter 5 for information on this topic.*]

32. Does the organization have effective procedures in place to ensure that donations or grants restricted for

specific purposes are actually used for such purposes? [*See Chapter 5 for information on this topic.*]

33. Does the board ensure that highly competent legal counsel reviews all of the organization's governing and policy documents and advises the board regarding their propriety? [*See Chapter 6 for information on this topic.*]

34. Does the organization maintain a proactive relationship with legal counsel in which legal counsel is engaged to review or draft all significant contractual documents that the organization plans to execute? [*See Chapter 7 for information on this topic.*]

35. Does the board engage in candid discussions in its meetings, even when the issues are difficult or uncomfortable? [*See Chapter 9 for information on this topic.*]

36. Are board members civil and respectful of the viewpoints of others during discussion and debate? [*See Chapter 9 for information on this topic.*]

37. Are there any aspects of the board's meetings or activities that are unusual and warrant specific discussion?

38. Are there other significant issues related to service on the organization's board that warrant discussion?

Suggestions for Further Reading

Managing the Nonprofit Organization – Principles and Practices by Peter F. Drucker (Collins Business)

Boards That Make a Difference (Third Edition) by John Carver (Jossey-Bass)

Good Governance for Nonprofits – Developing Principles and Policies for an Effective Board by Fredric L. Laughlin and Robert C. Andringa (AMACOM)

Nonprofit Risk Management & Contingency Planning – Done in a Day Strategies by Peggy M. Jackson (Wiley)

Robert's Rules of Order in Brief – The Simple Outline of the Rules Most Often Needed at a Meeting, According to the Standard Authoritative Parliamentary Manual (Revised Edition) by Henry M. Robert III, William J. Evans, Daniel H. Honemann, and Thomas J. Balch (Da Capo Press)

Donor-Restricted Gifts Simplified by Dan Busby (ECFA Press)

About the Author

Michael E. (Mike) Batts has served on, chaired, and consulted with nonprofit boards for more than 25 years. His board service has included serving as the board chairman for ECFA, a national nonprofit accrediting organization for religious nonprofit organizations in the areas of board governance and financial integrity. Mike was recently appointed chairman of the Commission on Accountability and Policy for Religious Organizations, a national commission convened upon the request of U.S. Senator Charles Grassley to address accountability and policy issues for U.S. religious organizations. Mike previously served on the Legal Framework Workgroup of the Panel on the Nonprofit Sector, an advisory panel to the U.S. Senate Finance Committee convened at the request of Senator Charles Grassley. He was first drawn to serving nonprofit organizations in response to his Christian faith and the need he saw among nonprofit organizations for guidance in the area of board governance and compliance.

Mike is also a CPA and the managing shareholder of Batts Morrison Wales & Lee, P.A., an Orlando-based CPA firm dedicated exclusively to serving nonprofit organizations and their affiliates throughout the United States.

Mike speaks throughout the country and writes frequently on topics related to the nonprofit sector. He is also active legislatively, having drafted and lobbied successfully for a number of changes to laws affecting nonprofit organizations.

83514070R00055

Made in the USA
San Bernardino, CA
26 July 2018